Andrew Jackson

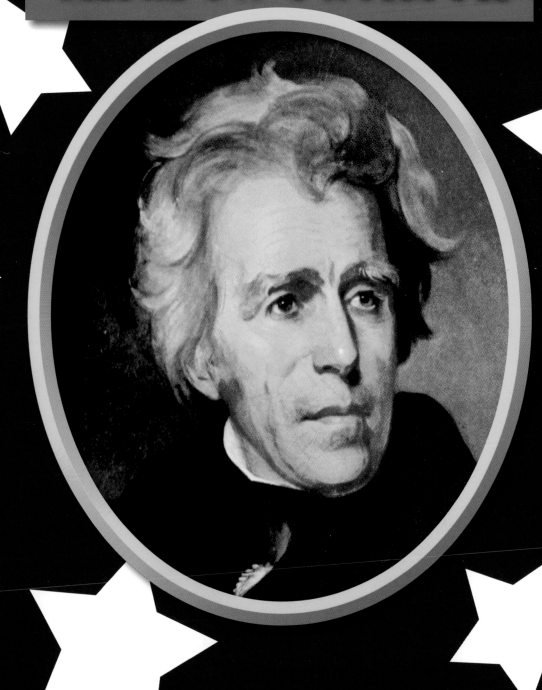

BY REBECCA RISSMAN

The Child's World®
childsworld.com

Published by The Child's World®
1980 Lookout Drive • Mankato, MN 56003-1705
800-599-READ • www.childsworld.com

ISBN 9781503816435
LCCN 2016945613

Printed in the United States of America
PAO2322

ABOUT THE AUTHOR

Rebecca Rissman is a nonfiction
author and editor. She has written
more than 200 books about history,
science, and art. She lives in Chicago,
Illinois, with her husband and two
daughters. She enjoys hiking, yoga,
and cooking.

Table of Contents

CHAPTER ONE

A Lasting Scar 5

CHAPTER TWO

Successful Businessman 9

CHAPTER THREE

War Hero 13

CHAPTER FOUR

The Frontier President 17

Timeline 22

Glossary 23

To Learn More 24

Index 24

The Revolutionary War lasted from 1775 to 1783.

A Lasting Scar

Andrew Jackson was young when the Revolutionary War began. It was 1775. Andrew was only eight years old. The war was between Great Britain and the American **colonies**. The colonies were the new settled areas in North America. They would one day form the United States. The colonies were ruled by the British. They paid **taxes** to Britain. But they did not get a say in British government. Many colonists did not think this was fair. They wanted to break away from Britain.

Andrew lived in North Carolina. He was angry with the British. His mother died because of the war. His two brothers died too. Andrew wanted to help fight. He joined the armed forces. Then British troops attacked Andrew's hometown in 1780.

British soldiers took Andrew prisoner. He was only 13 years old. A British officer wanted his shoes shined. He asked Andrew to do it. But Andrew said no. The officer became angry. He hit Andrew in the face with his sword. This left Andrew with a scar. Andrew was freed two weeks later.

Andrew hated the British his whole life. He never forgot how the war changed his family. His scar reminded him how the British treated him. His time as a prisoner made him strong. He had to be brave. One day, as president, Andrew would be strong again.

Jackson is the only president to have been held as a prisoner of war.

Jackson was born in an area called the Waxhaws, which is somewhere between North and South Carolina.

CHAPTER TWO

Successful Businessman

Andrew Jackson was born on March 15, 1767. He lived far out in the country. His home was west of most settled cities. People called this area the **frontier**. Jackson's family was poor. He had little education. He was known for being wild. He loved fighting and playing tricks on people.

The British attack changed Jackson's life. Jackson went on to study law. He became a successful lawyer.

In 1794, Jackson got married. His wife's name was Rachel Donelson.

Then in 1796 Jackson joined politics. He was elected to the U.S. House of Representatives. In 1797 he was chosen for the U.S. **Senate**. He helped make laws in these positions. The next year he became a judge.

Jackson was a hard worker. He owned many small businesses. He ran a general store. He also owned racetracks for horses. Jackson made a lot of money. He bought a large **plantation** in Tennessee.

Jackson was a tough man. He often got in fights. Once Jackson **dueled** a man. The man shot Jackson in the chest. But Jackson did not flinch. He shot back at the man. The man died. Jackson never showed that he was hurt. The bullet stayed in him for the rest of his life.

It's estimated that Jackson fought as many as 5 to 100 duels.

Jackson became well-known. People thought of him as a leader. They also knew that he became angry easily. But he was mostly known for his successful businesses.

Jackson was nicknamed "Old Hickory" for his determination and concern for other soldiers.

CHAPTER THREE

War Hero

Jackson became an important U.S. **military** figure. He was a leader in the War of 1812. This war was between the United States and England. The war had many causes. The British stopped Americans from trading with other countries. They also helped Native Americans fight American settlers. Americans decided to go to war. Canada and some Native Americans fought for the British. They wanted to stop Americans from moving west. Other Native Americans fought with the U.S. forces.

Jackson helped the United States win the war. He led soldiers in the Battle at Horseshoe Bend. U.S. forces were fighting Native Americans. Jackson's troops were fierce. They outnumbered the Native Americans. Jackson's men attacked from the front and back. They won the battle.

In 1815, Jackson went to New Orleans, Louisiana. The British were about to take over the city. Jackson wanted to stop them. He needed a large army. He asked U.S. soldiers and other Native Americans to fight. He also asked free African Americans and even pirates. The British attacked. Jackson's men fought bravely. They beat the British. They kept the British out of New Orleans.

Jackson became a hero. He was very popular. He decided he wanted to run for president. He ran in 1824. But he did not win.

The Battle of New Orleans was the final major conflict in the War of 1812.

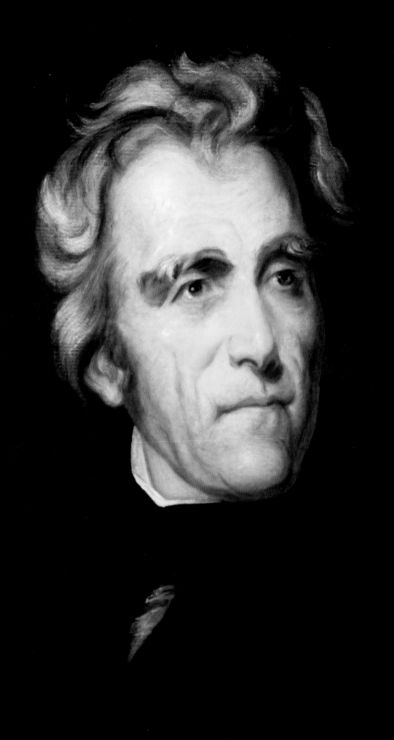

Jackson was the first president from Tennessee.

CHAPTER FOUR

The Frontier President

Jackson ran for president again in 1828. He ran against John Quincy Adams. Adams was the current president. This time Jackson won. He was America's first "frontier president."

Jackson had firm beliefs. He thought the president alone was in charge. Other presidents worked with Congress to make decisions. But Jackson did not. He wanted to make his own choices.

Jackson had other strong **opinions**. He thought states' rights were very important. He also allowed **slavery**. He even wanted it to spread to more states.

The Bank of the United States was a business. It helped the government store its money. Jackson thought the bank was a problem. He thought it only helped the rich. But Congress liked the bank. It voted for a bill to keep using it. Jackson turned down the bill. It was a bold move. Jackson wanted to run for president again. He knew some voters liked the bank. They would be angry with his choice. He could lose their votes. Many people voted for him anyway. Jackson was reelected in 1832.

Jackson also had ideas about Native Americans. The Cherokee nation lived on good farming land in Georgia. They had been there for many years. But Jackson wanted that land for the United States.

Native Americans were forced to move to the land that is now Oklahoma.

He also thought there was gold there. So he told the government to take the land. He wanted the Cherokee moved west. Some **tribes** traded their old land. In return they received land in the west. But most refused to leave.

The government forced the Native Americans off their land. They had to walk thousands of miles. The conditions were horrible. Thousands died. This was known as the "Trail of Tears."

Jackson left the White House in 1837. He moved back to Tennessee. His plantation produced cotton. It also made butter and other goods. Jackson owned more than 150 slaves.

Jackson enjoyed life at home. He still helped people in politics. He even helped the next president. But Jackson's health started to fail. He died at his home in 1845.

Jackson was a strong leader. Some remember him as a war hero. To others he is known for owning slaves. But most know how he treated Native Americans. People remember how he caused the "Trail of Tears."

Jackson was 78 years old when he died.

1760

←— **March 15, 1767** Andrew Jackson is born.

←— **1775–1783** The Revolutionary War is fought.

←— **1796** Jackson is elected to the U.S. House of Representatives.

←— **1797** Jackson is chosen for the U.S. Senate.

←— **1812–1815** War of 1812 is fought between Great Britain and the United States.

←— **March 27, 1814** Jackson leads the U.S. forces in their victory at the Battle of Horseshoe Bend.

←— **January 8, 1815** Jackson leads the U.S. forces in their victory at the Battle of New Orleans.

←— **1828** Jackson is elected president.

←— **1832** Jackson is reelected president.

←— **July 10, 1832** Jackson vetoes a bill that would have supported the Bank of the United States.

←— **1838–1839** More than 15,000 Native Americans are forced to travel to their new land on the "Trail of Tears."

←— **June 8, 1845** Jackson dies in his home in Tennessee.

1850

colonies (KOL-uh-nees) Colonies are large areas of land that are ruled by another country. Jackson fought for the American colonies against the British in the Revolutionary War.

dueled (DOO-uhled) When two people have dueled, they have fought using strict rules about the method of fighting. Jackson dueled a man using a gun.

frontier (fruhn-TIHR) The frontier is the far edge of a country, often where not many people live. Jackson was born on the frontier.

military (MIL-uh-ter-ee) The military is a group made up of armed forces. Jackson was an important military leader.

opinions (uh-PIN-yuhns) Opinions are personal views or beliefs. Jackson had strong opinions about states' rights.

plantation (plan-TAY-shun) A plantation is a large farm. Jackson's plantation grew cotton.

Senate (SEN-it) The U.S. Senate is the smaller of two groups that form the U.S. Congress. Jackson was chosen for the Senate in 1797.

slavery (SLAY-vuh-ree) Slavery is when someone owns and controls another person. Jackson supported slavery.

taxes (TAKS-is) Taxes are money that people and companies pay to the government. American colonists did not want to pay taxes to the British.

tribes (TRIBES) Tribes are groups of people, typically families, who share the same customs and beliefs. Jackson forced many Native American tribes off their land.

In the Library

Gaines, Ann Graham. *Andrew Jackson*. Mankato,
MN: The Child's World, 2009.

Hunsicker, Jennifer. *Young Andrew Jackson in the Carolinas:
A Revolutionary Boy*. Charleston, SC: The History Press, 2014.

Wilson, Steve. *Andrew Jackson's Presidency: Democracy
in Action*. New York: PowerKids Press, 2016.

On the Web

Visit our Web site for links about Andrew Jackson: **childsworld.com/links**

*Note to Parents, Teachers, and Librarians: We routinely verify our Web links to make
sure they are safe and active sites. So encourage your readers to check them out!*

INDEX

Bank of the United States, 18
Battle at Horseshoe Bend, 14
British, 5-6, 9, 13-14

Congress, 17, 18

frontier, 9, 17

Native Americans, 13-14, 18-20
New Orleans, Louisiana, 14

prisoner, 6

Revolutionary War, 5

Tennessee, 10, 20
Trail of Tears, 20

War of 1812, 13